MO MOOLAH

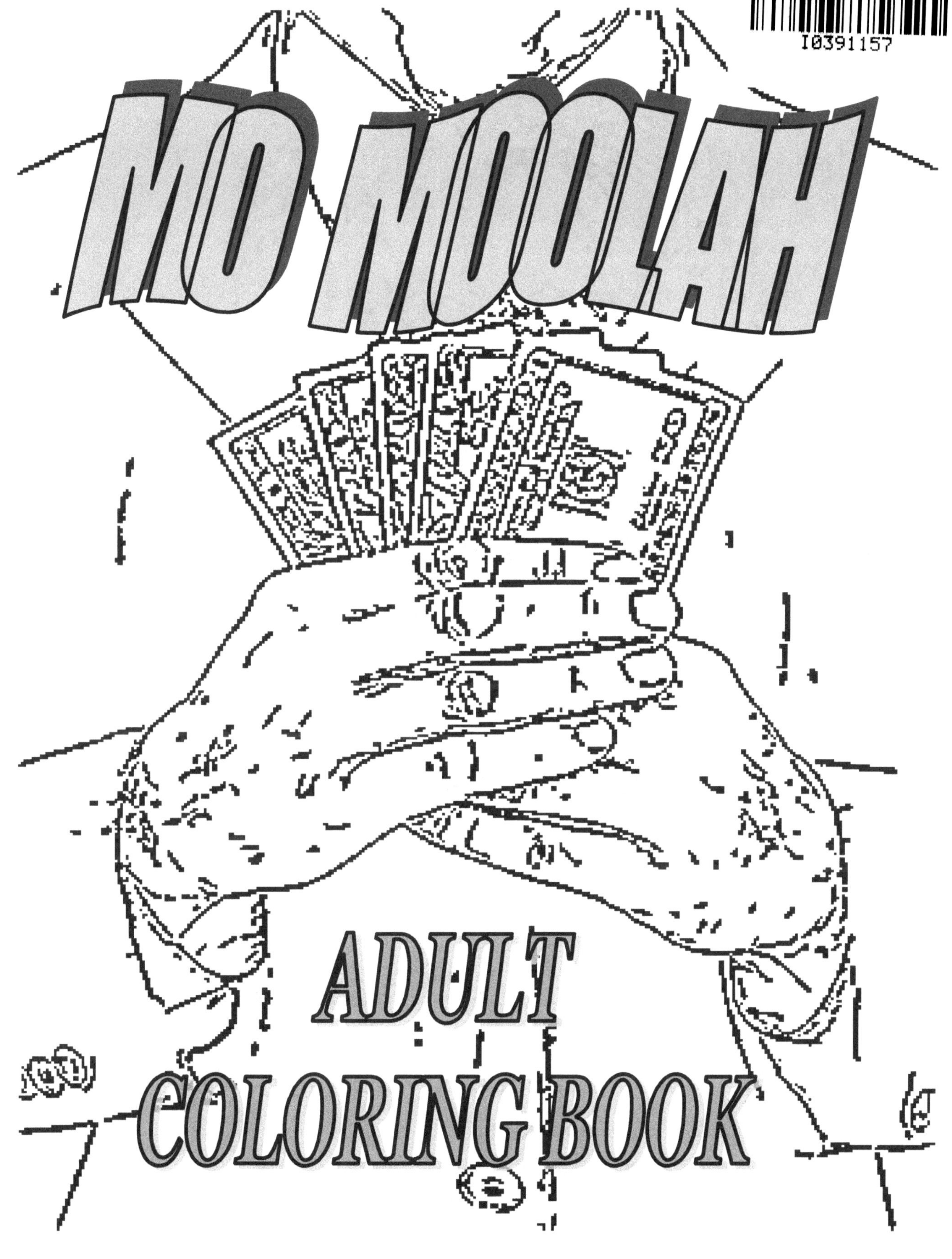

ADULT COLORING BOOK

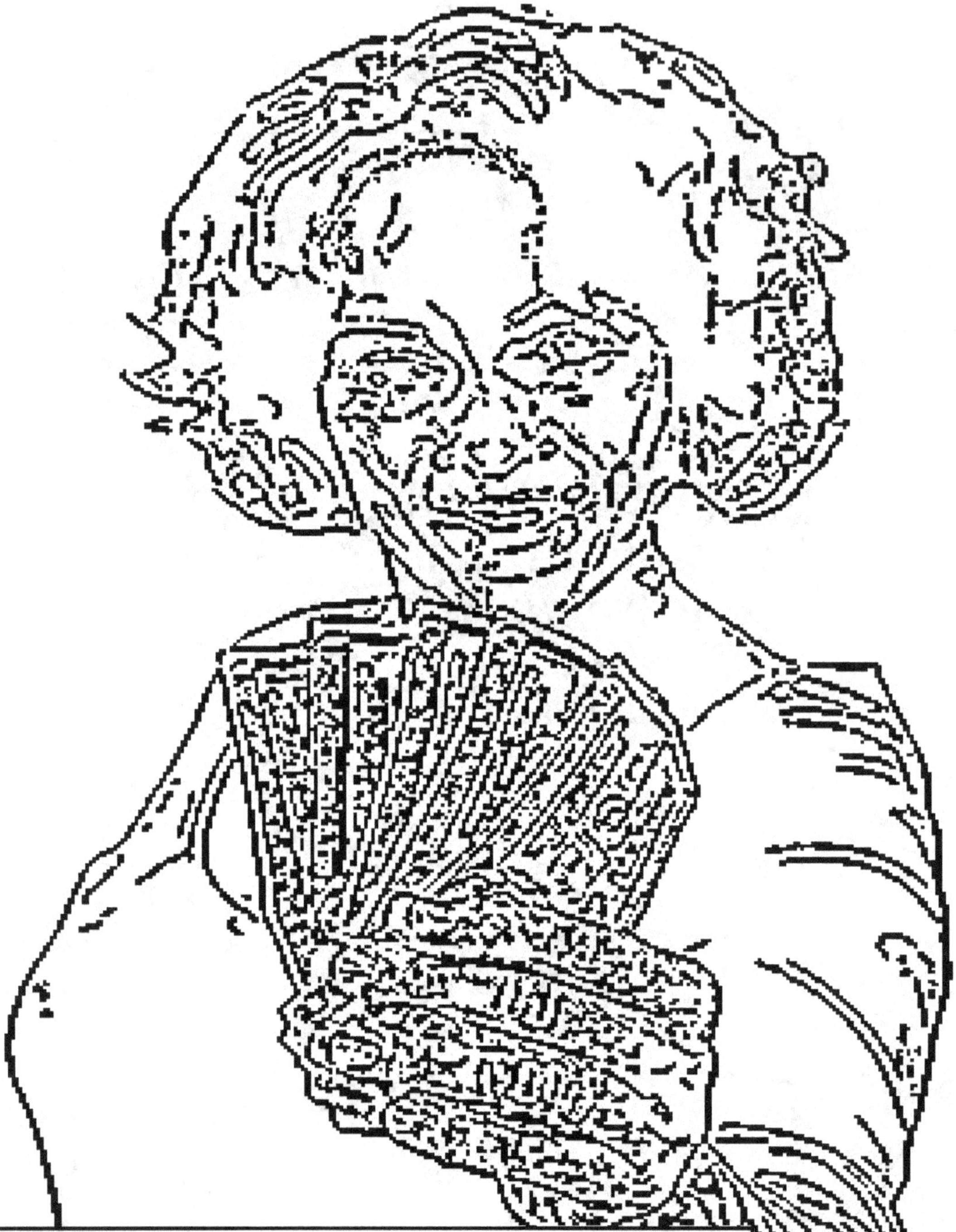

MO MOOLAH

Printed in the United States of America

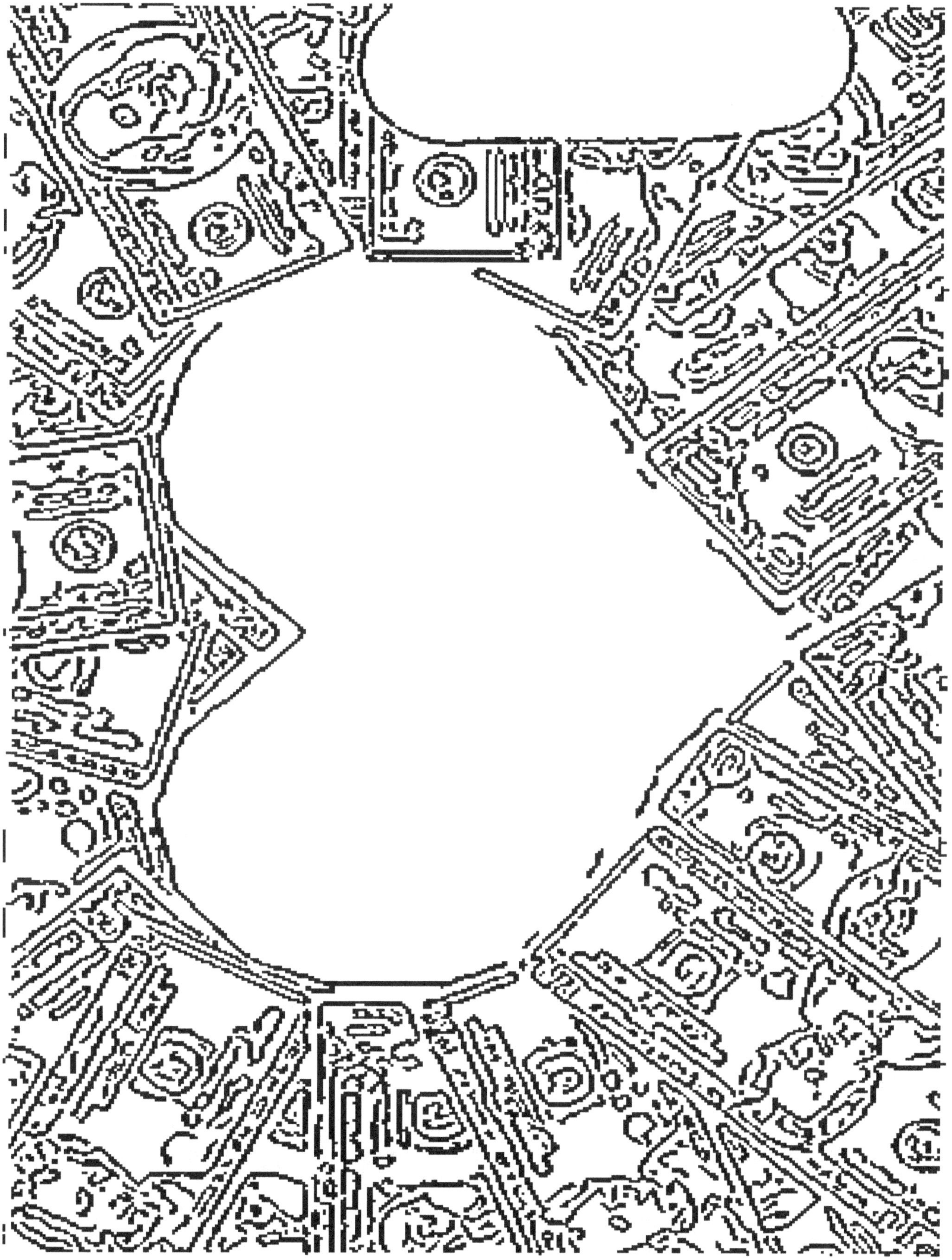

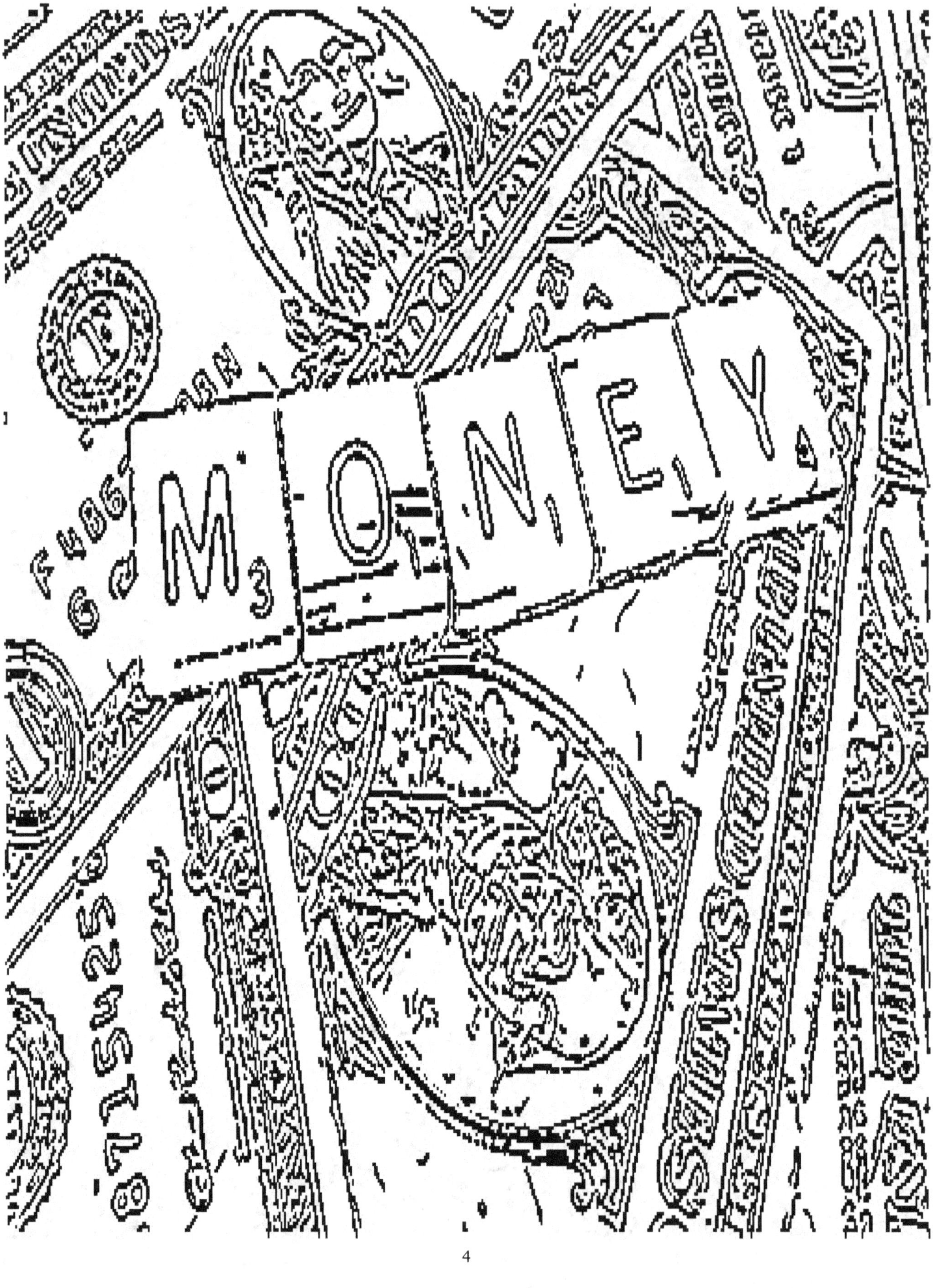
MONEY

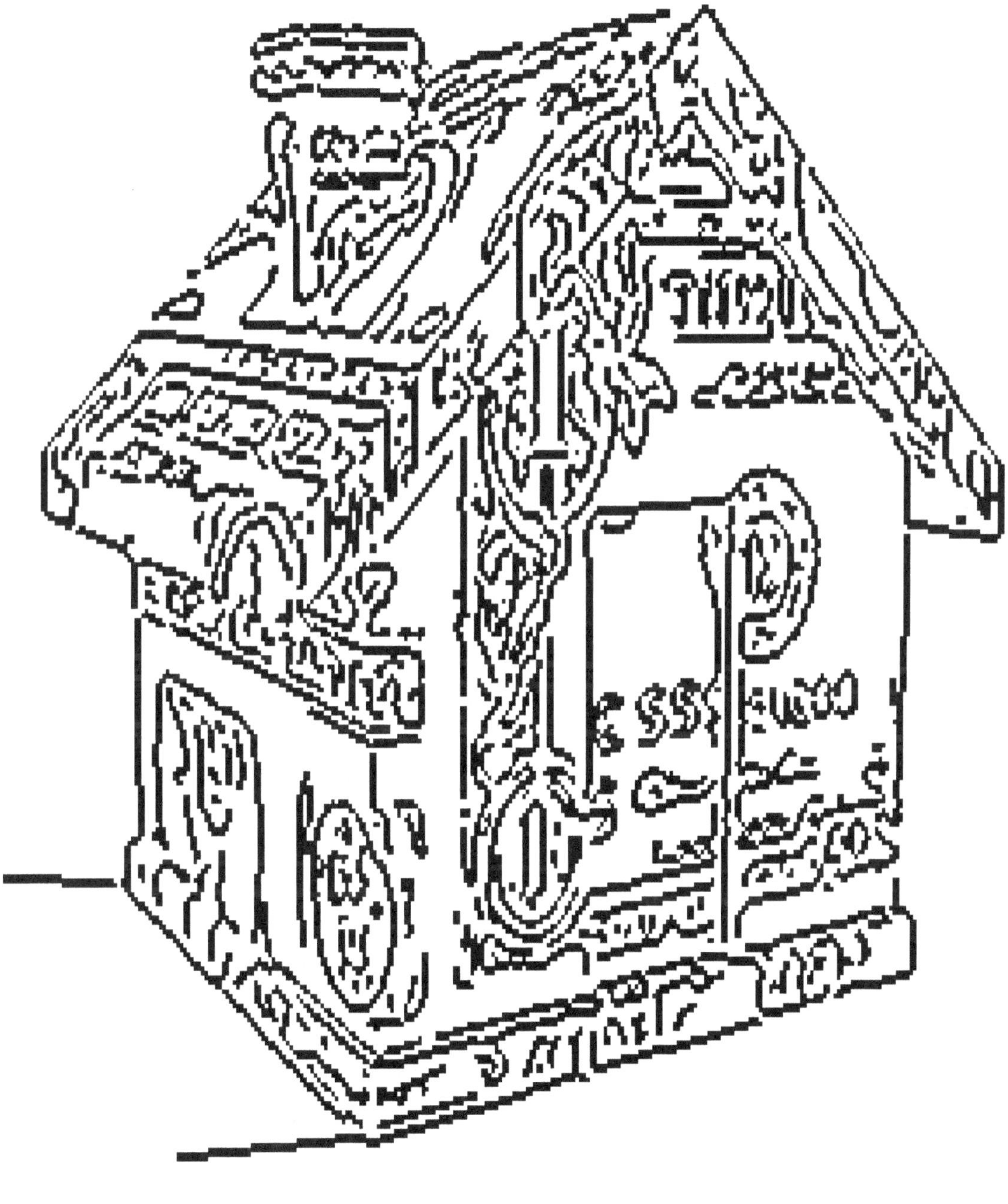

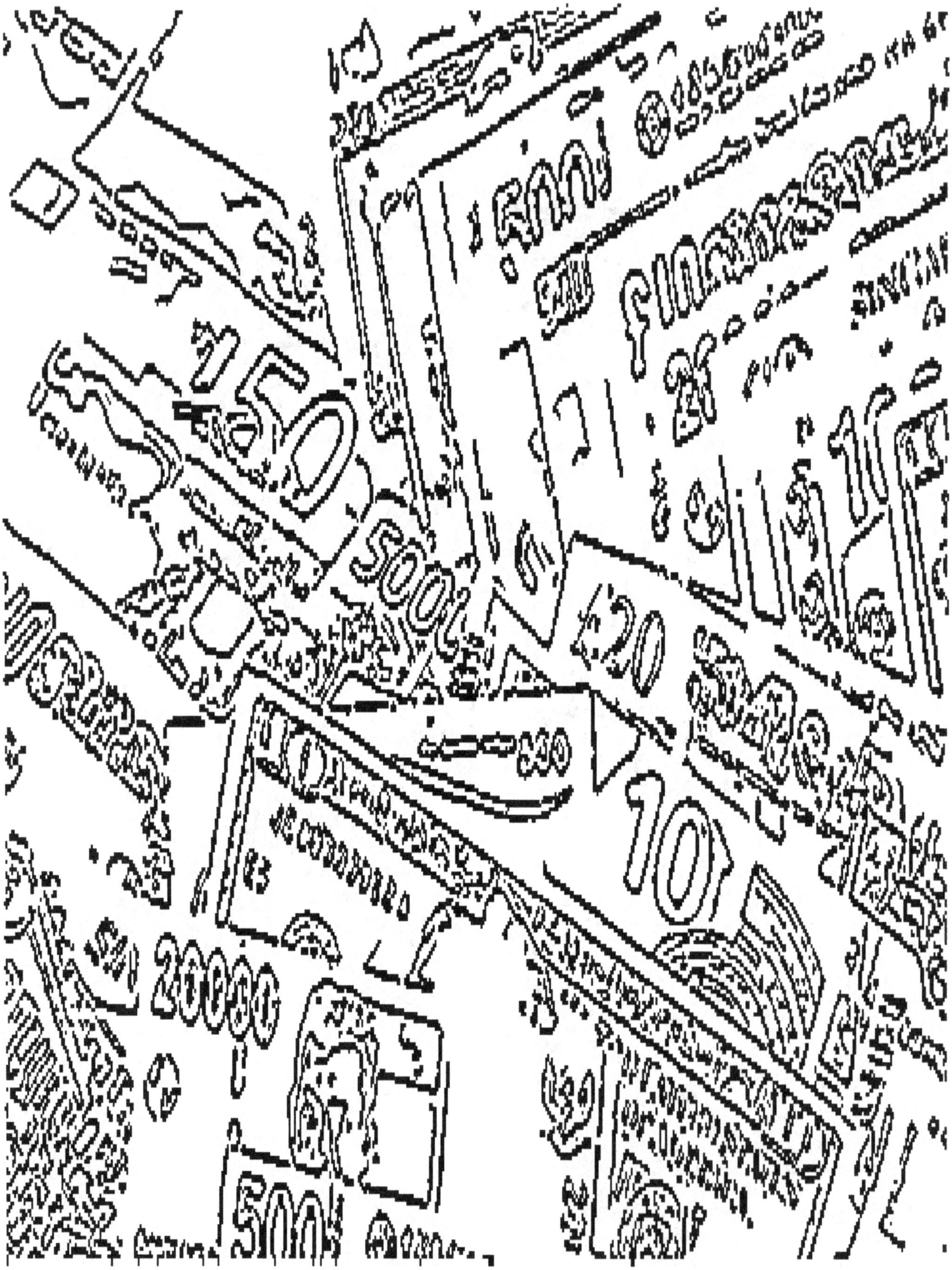

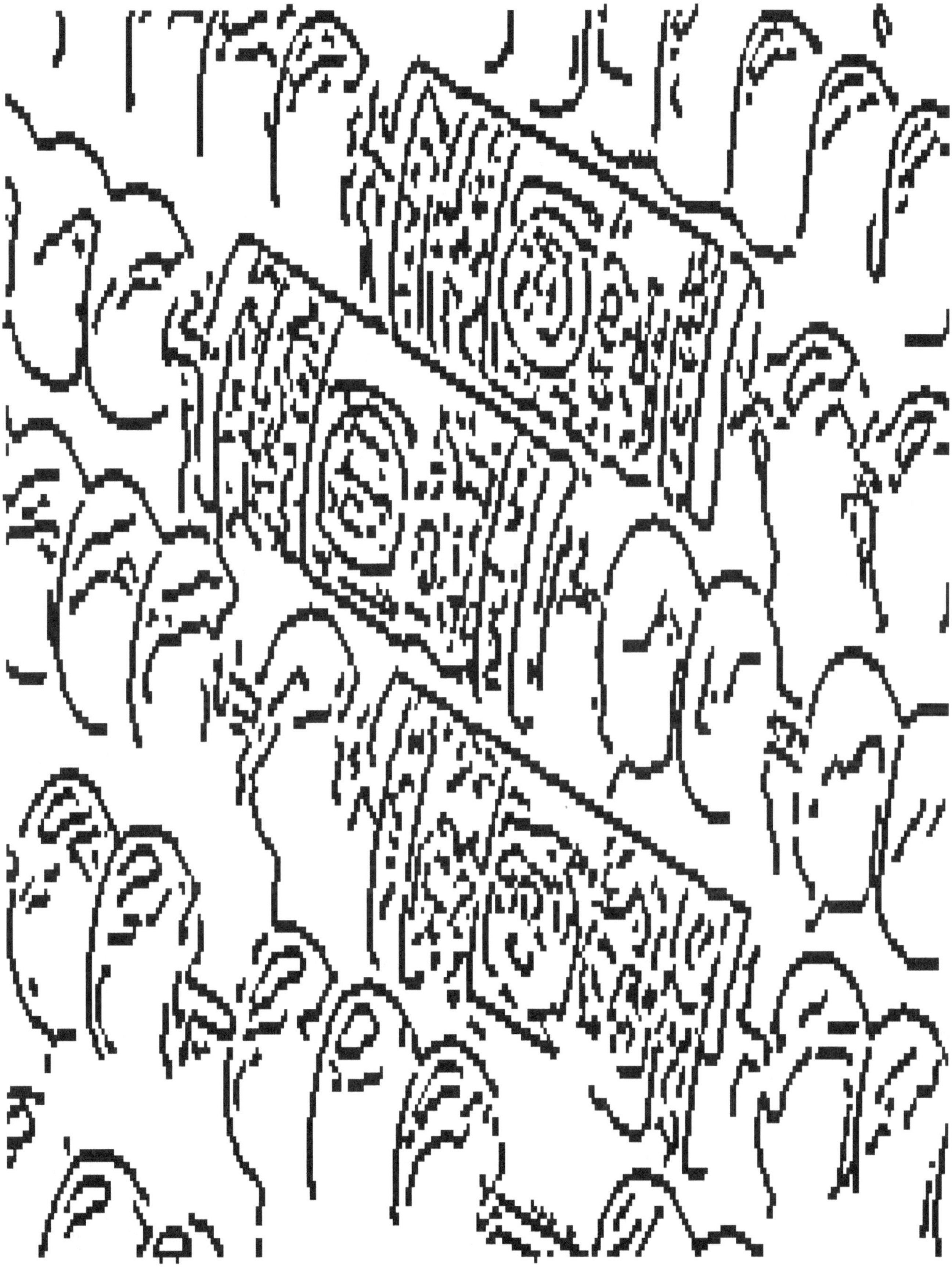

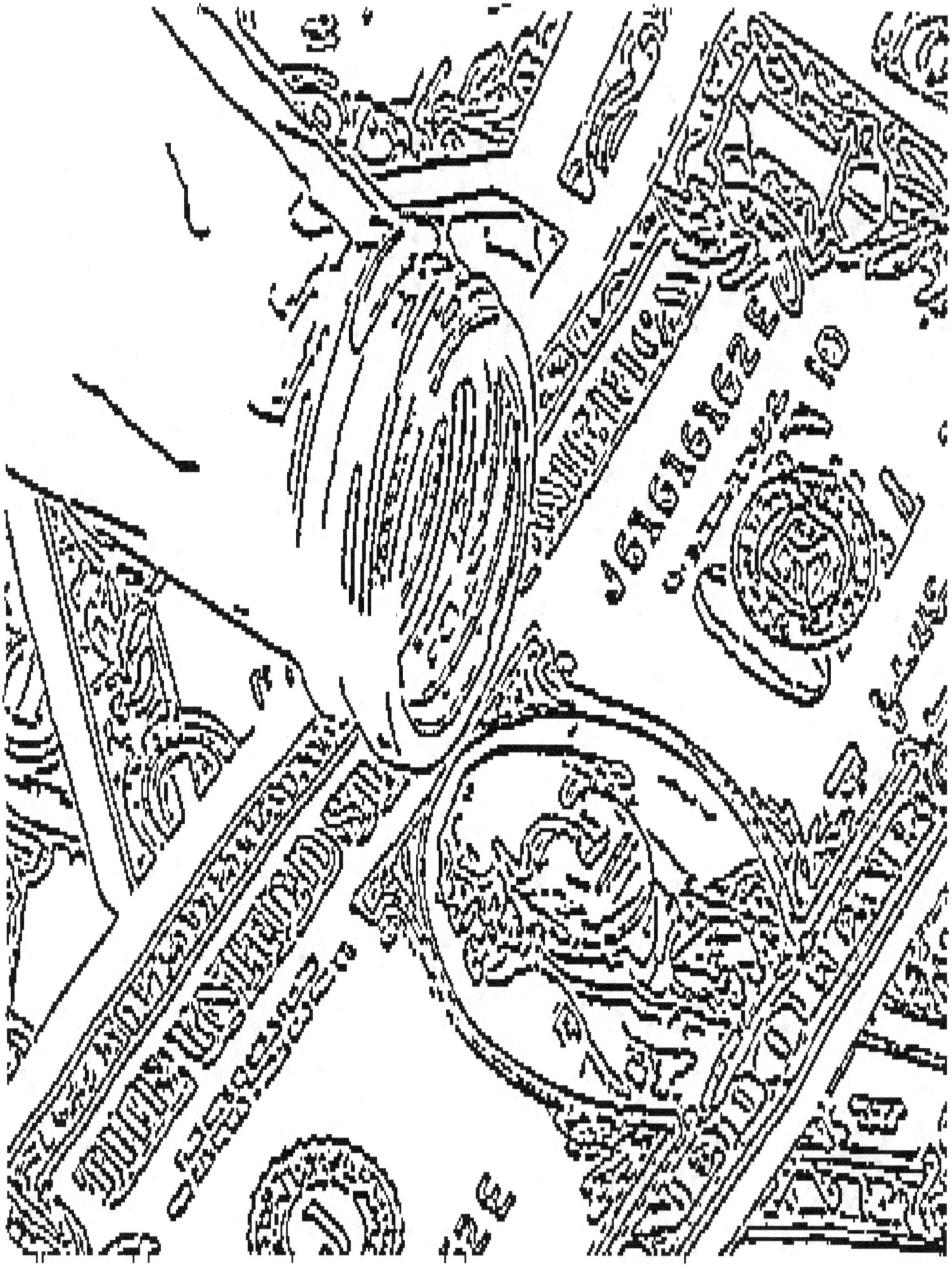

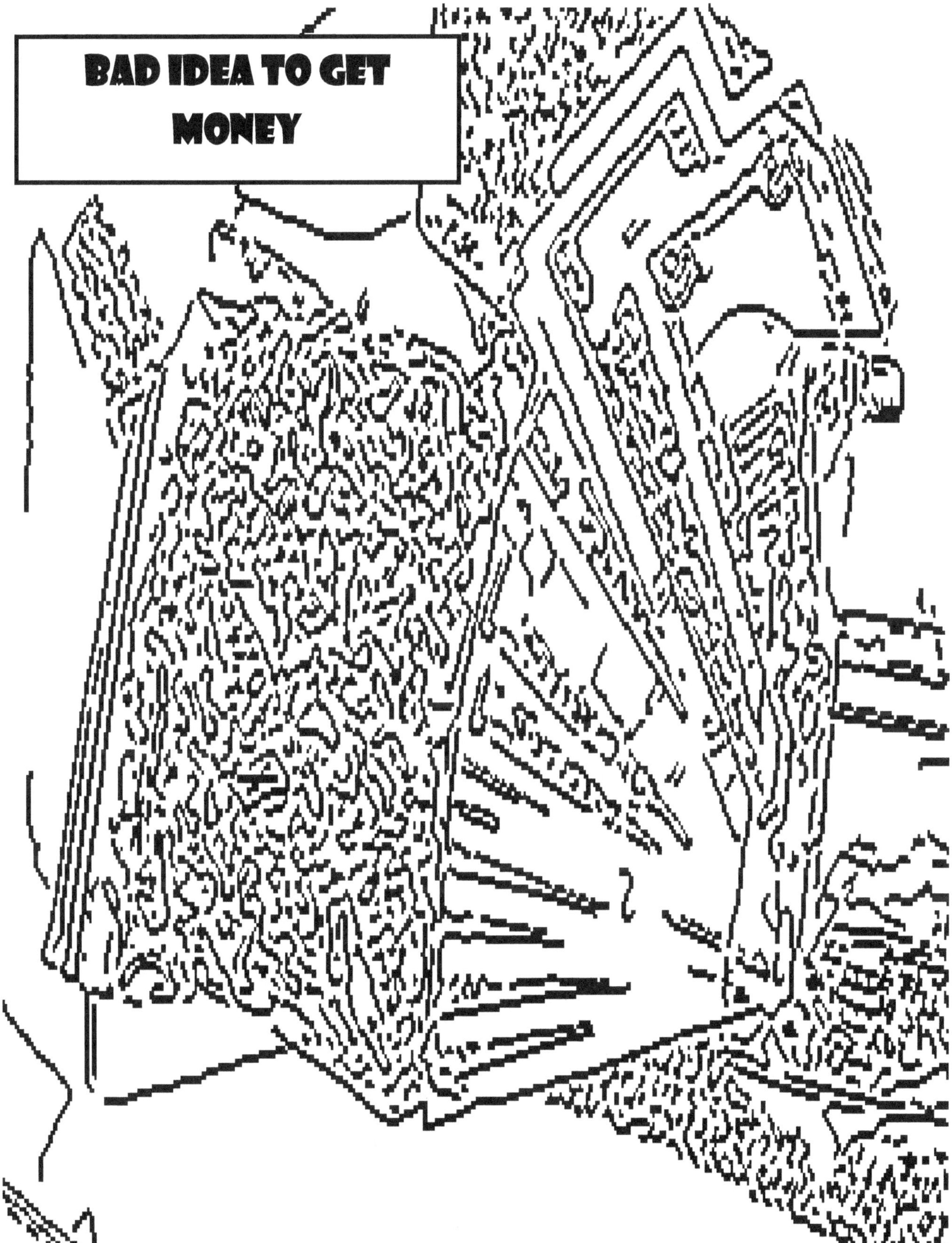
BAD IDEA TO GET MONEY

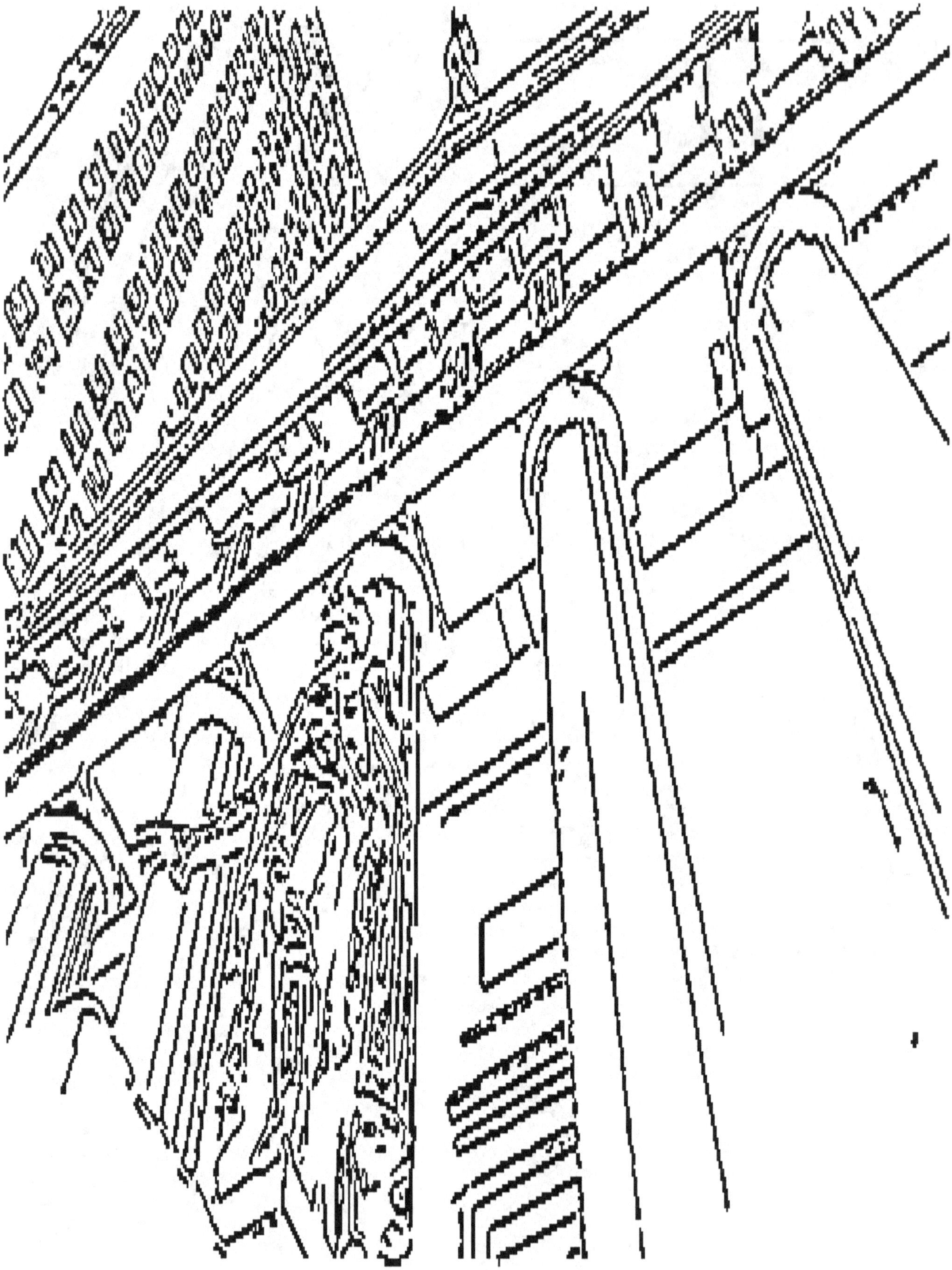

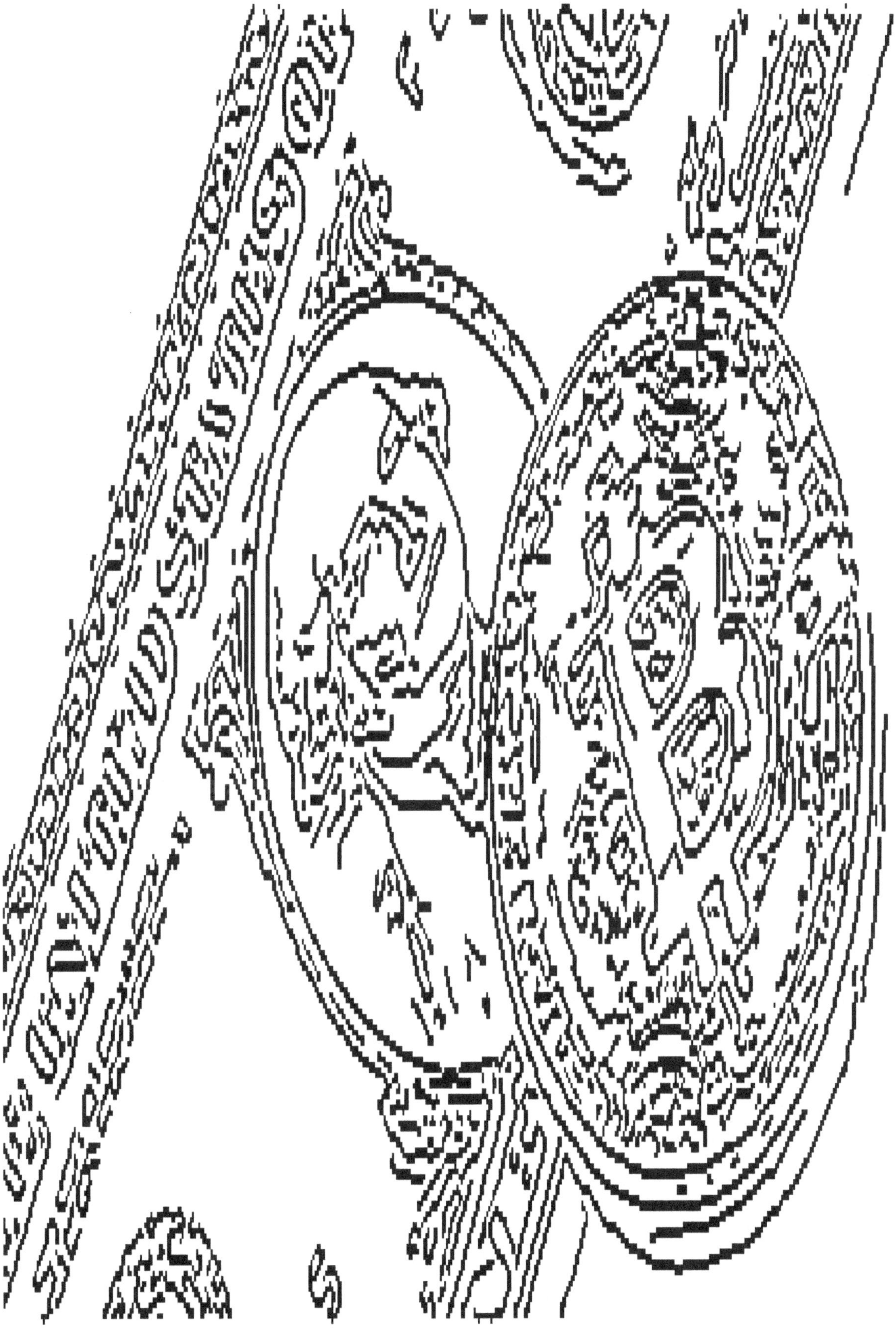

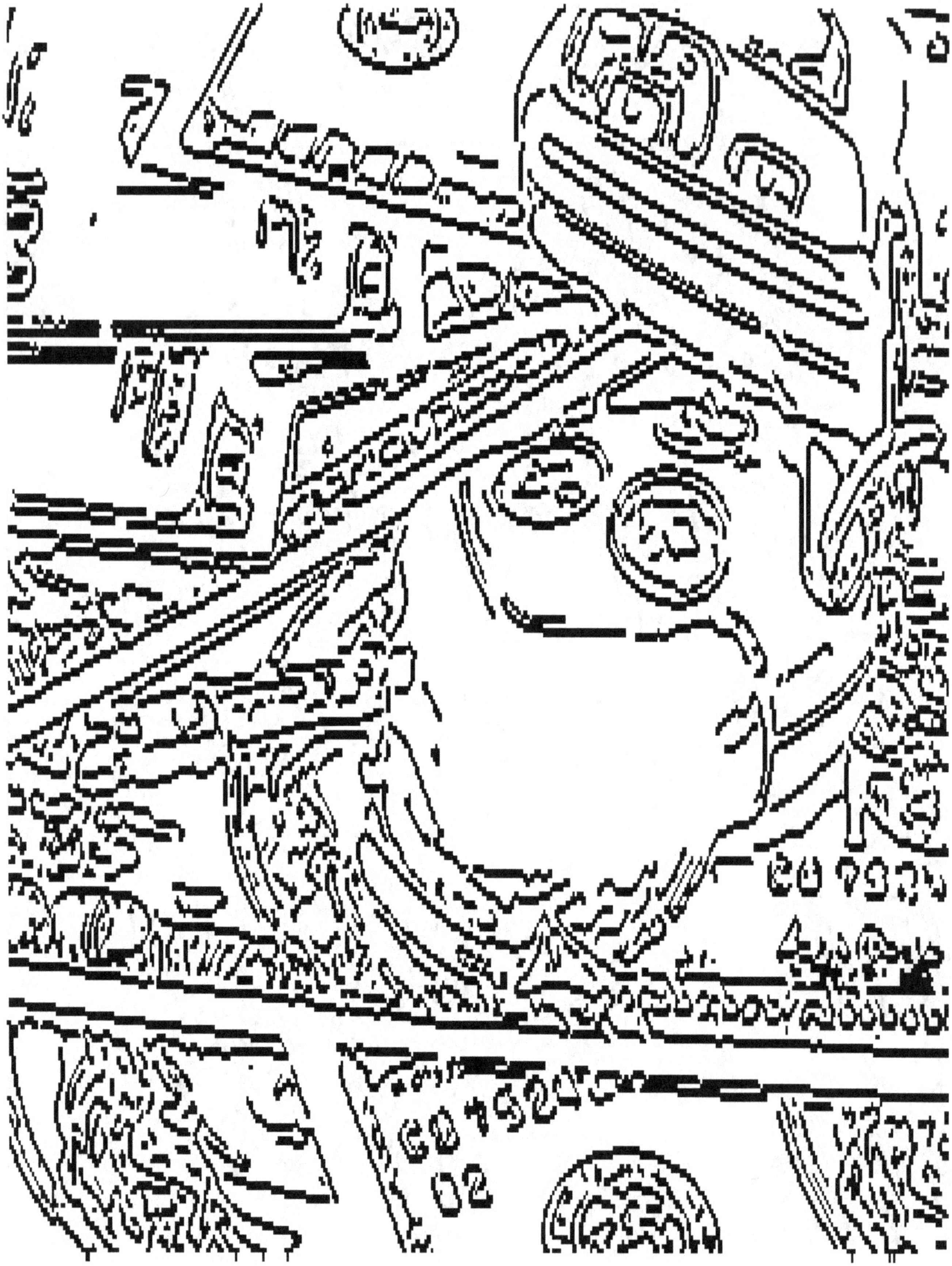

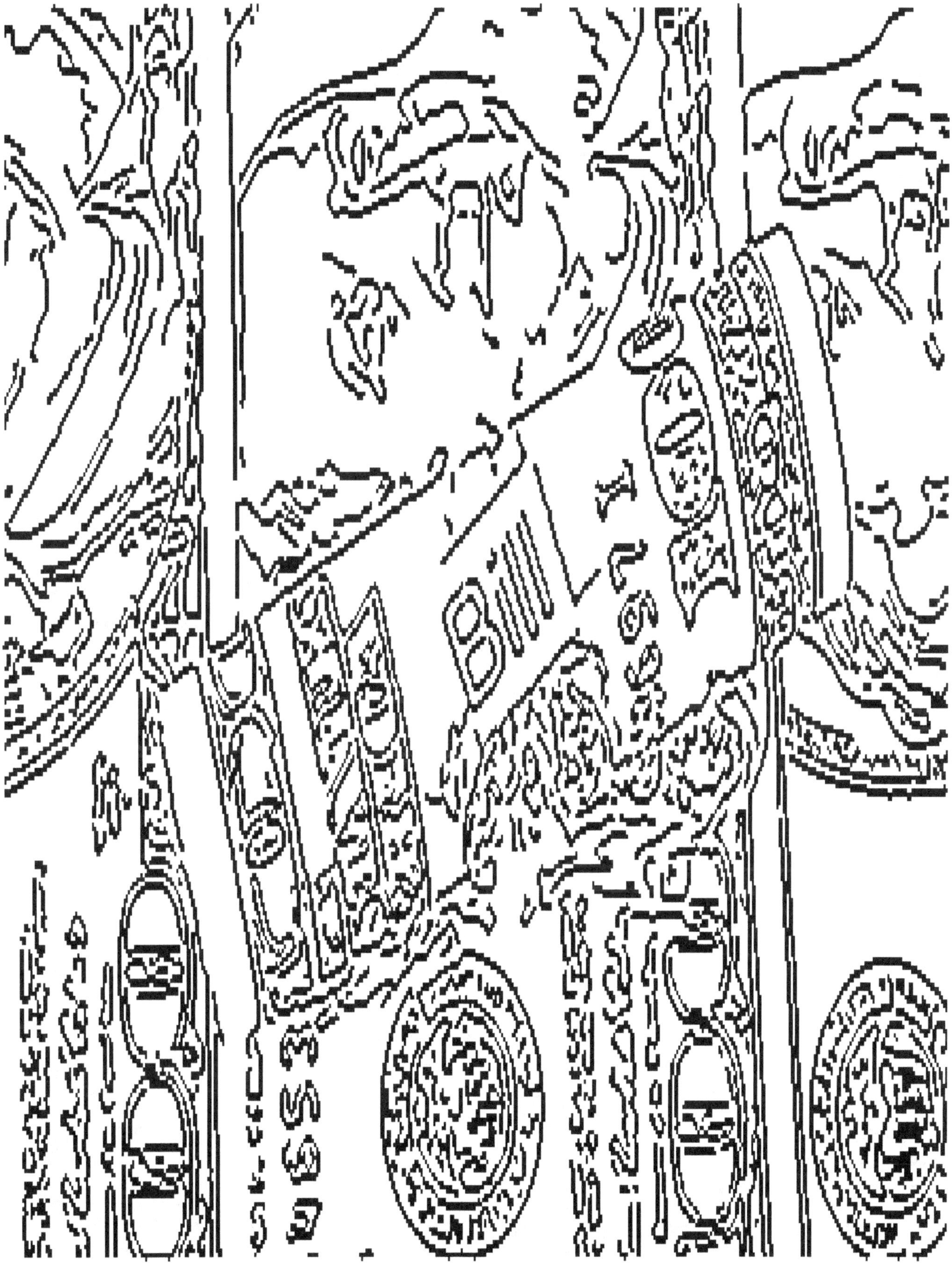
Bill

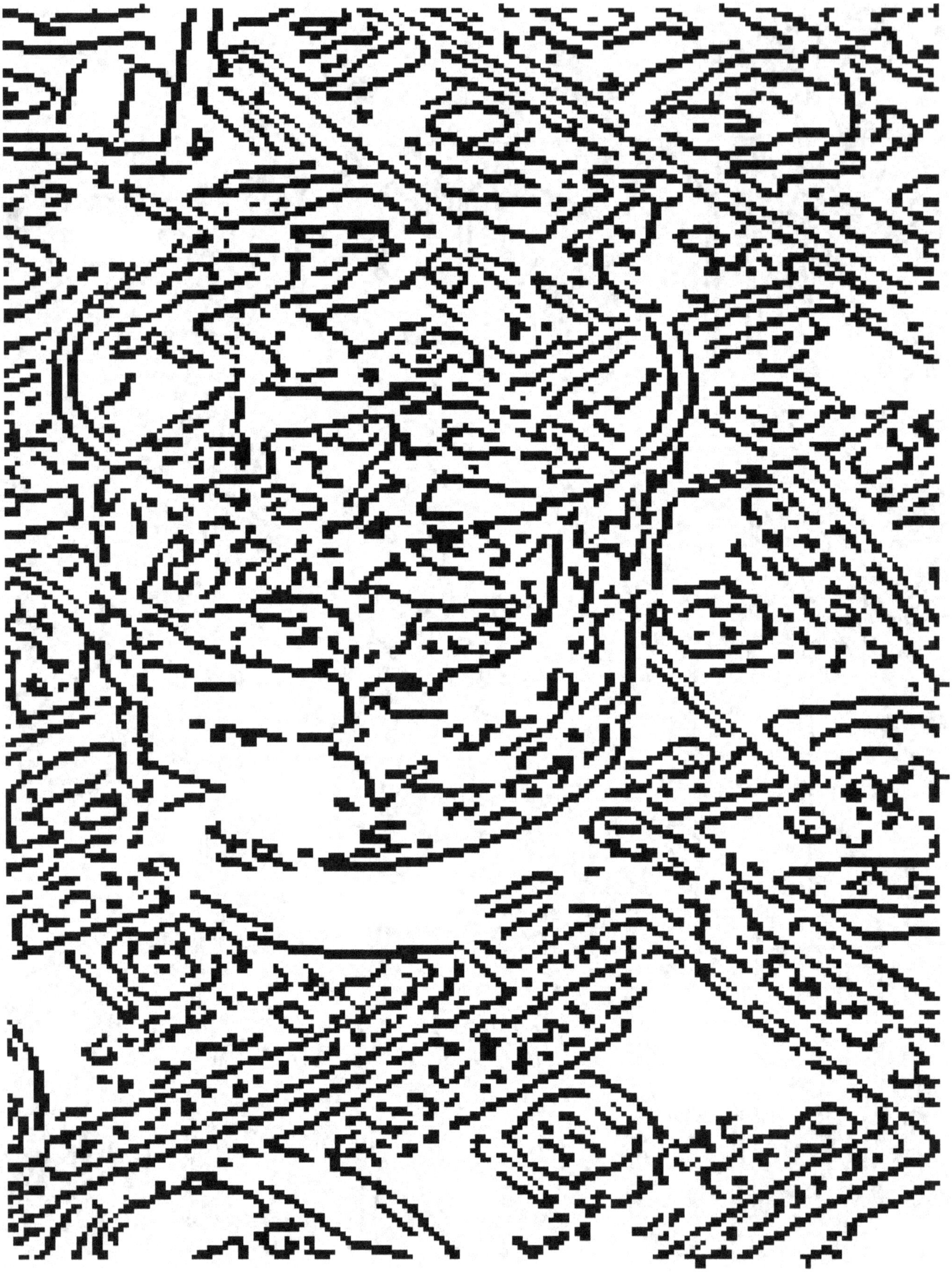

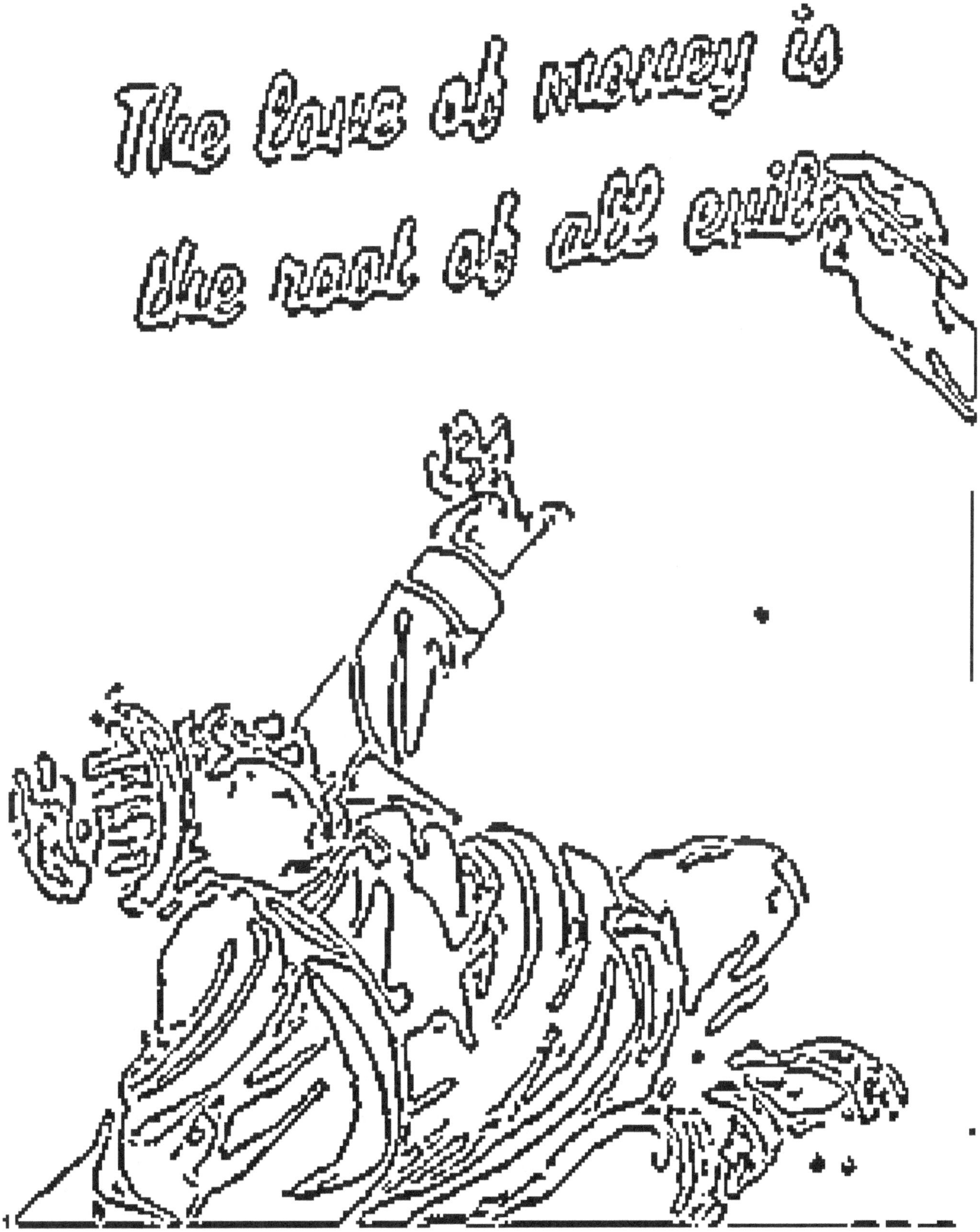
The love of money is
the root of all evil

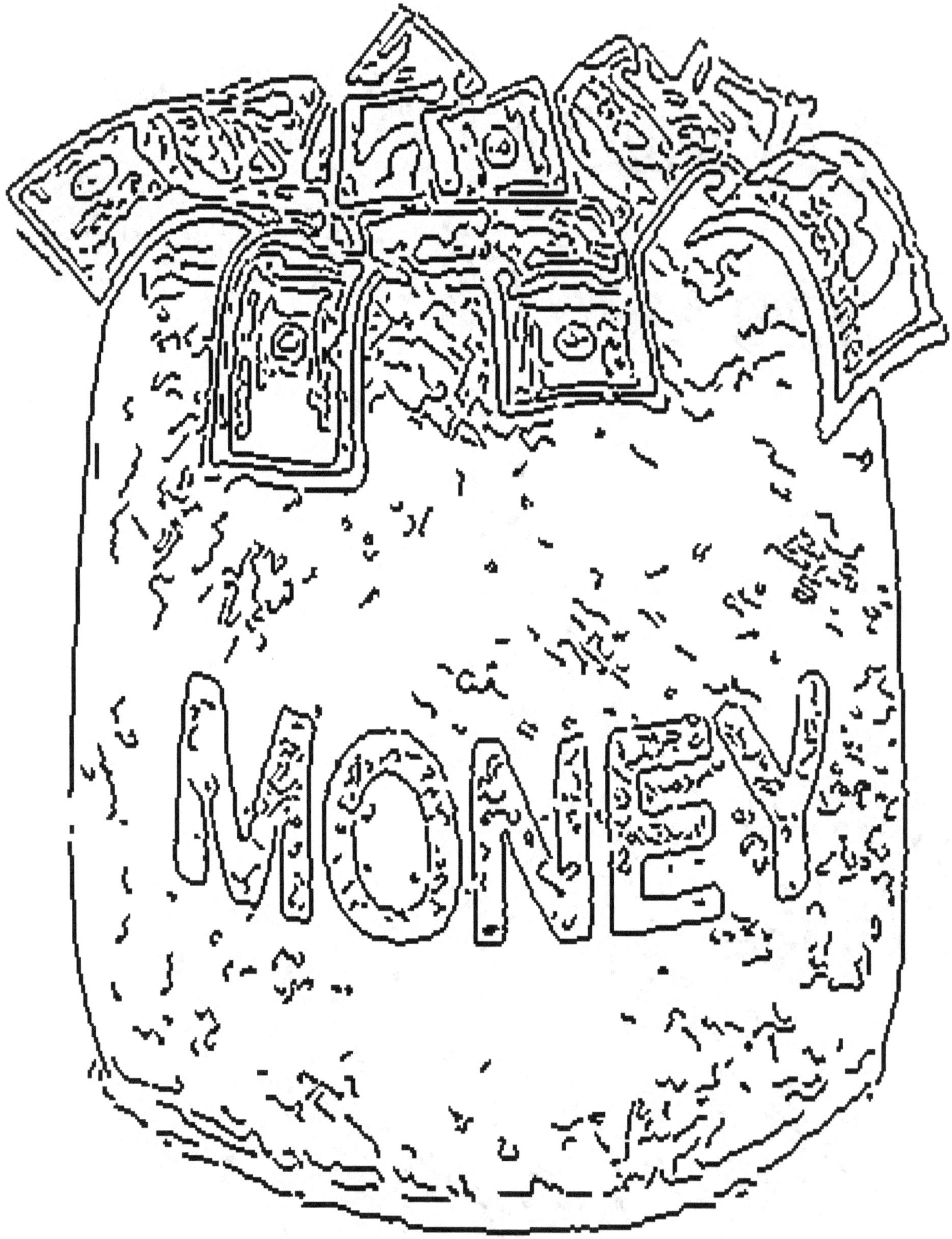
MONEY

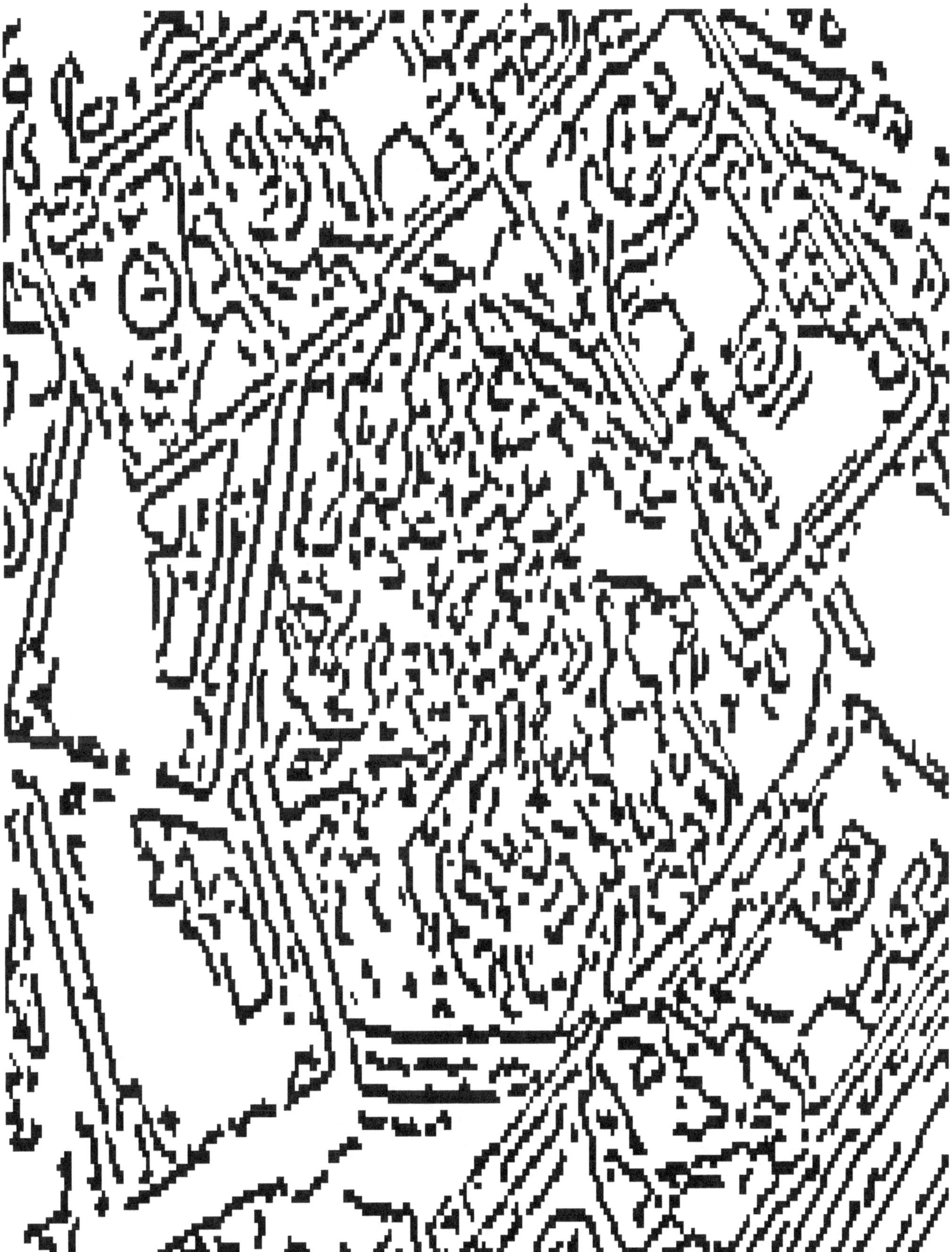

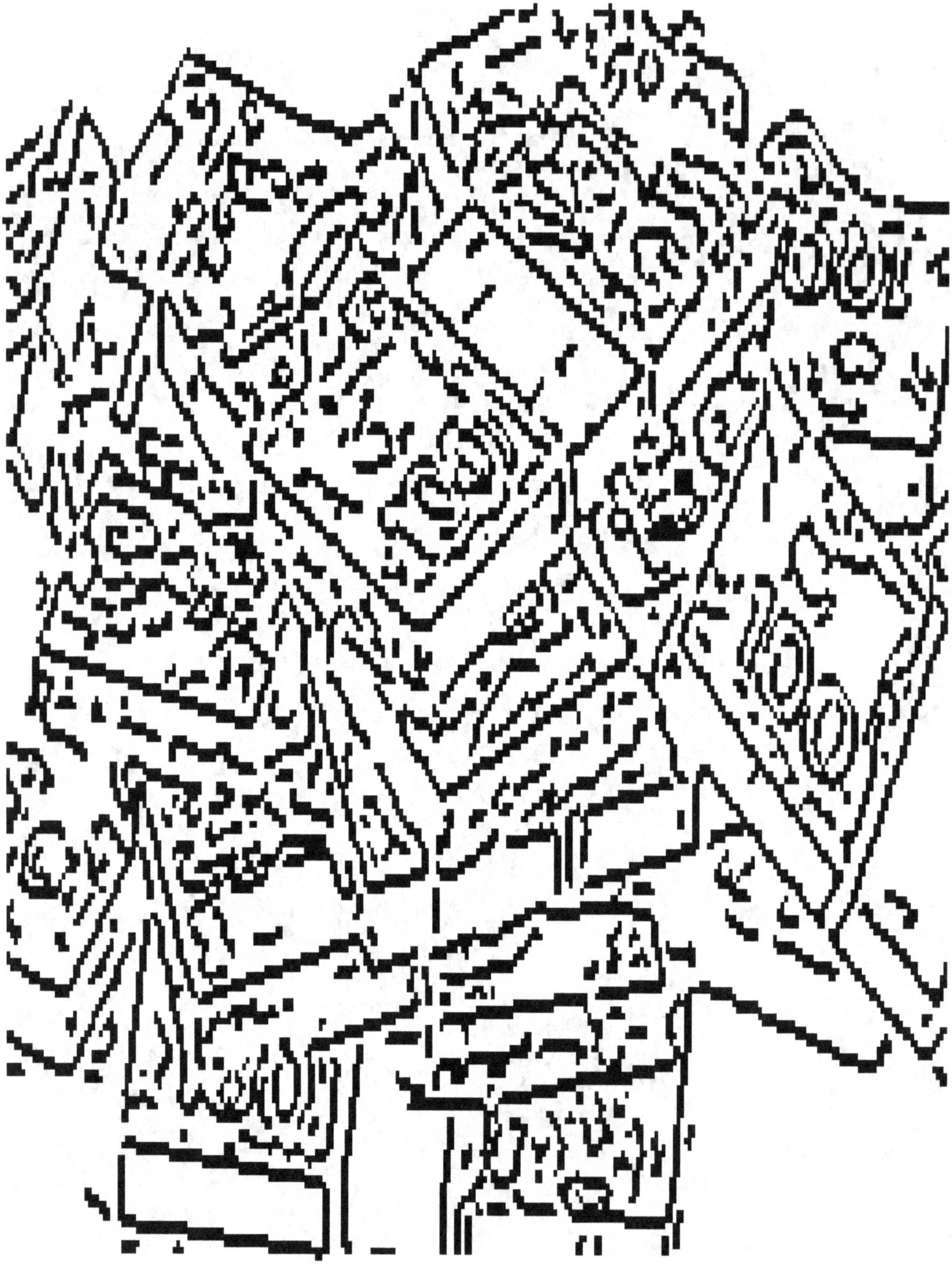

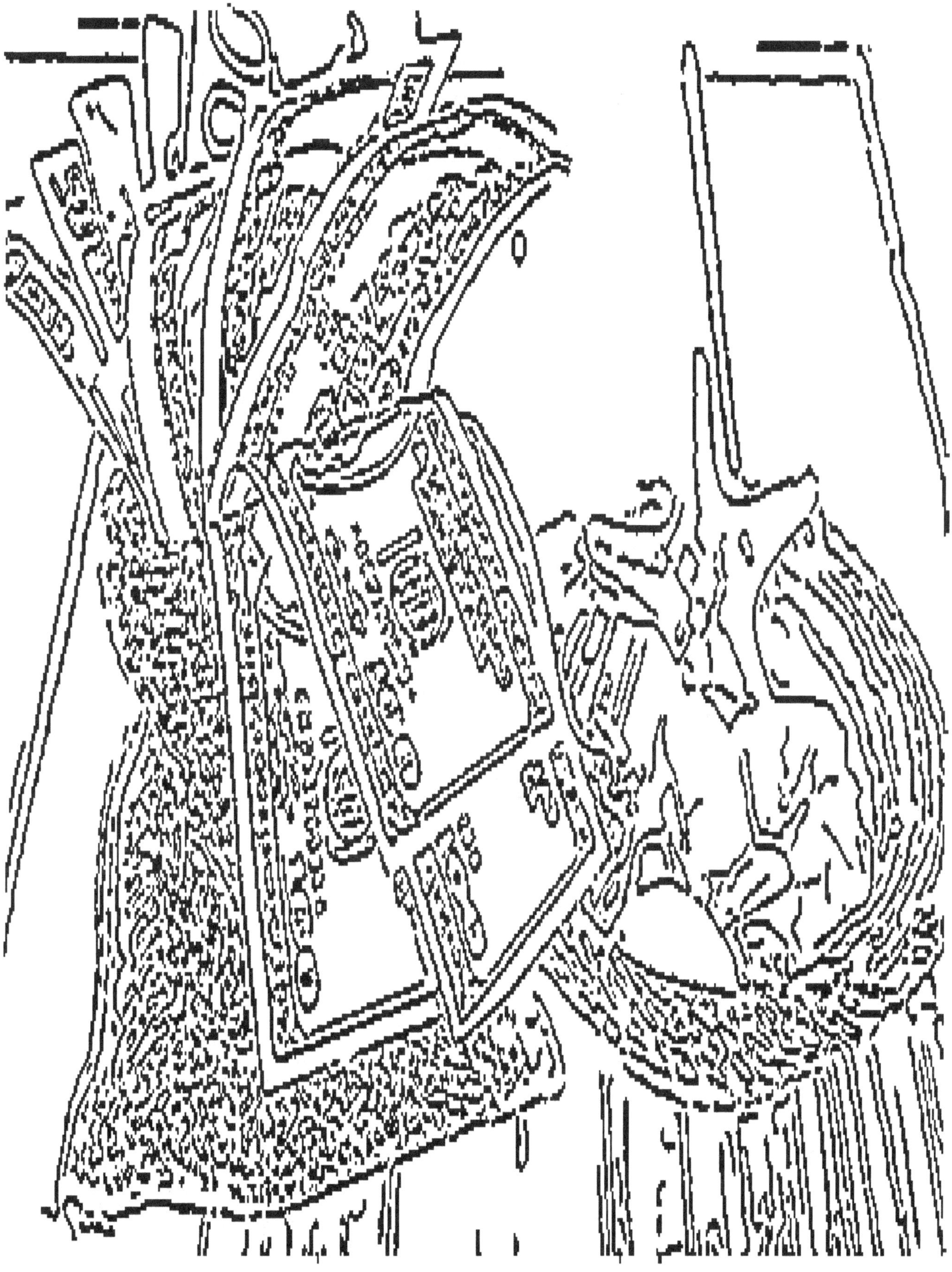

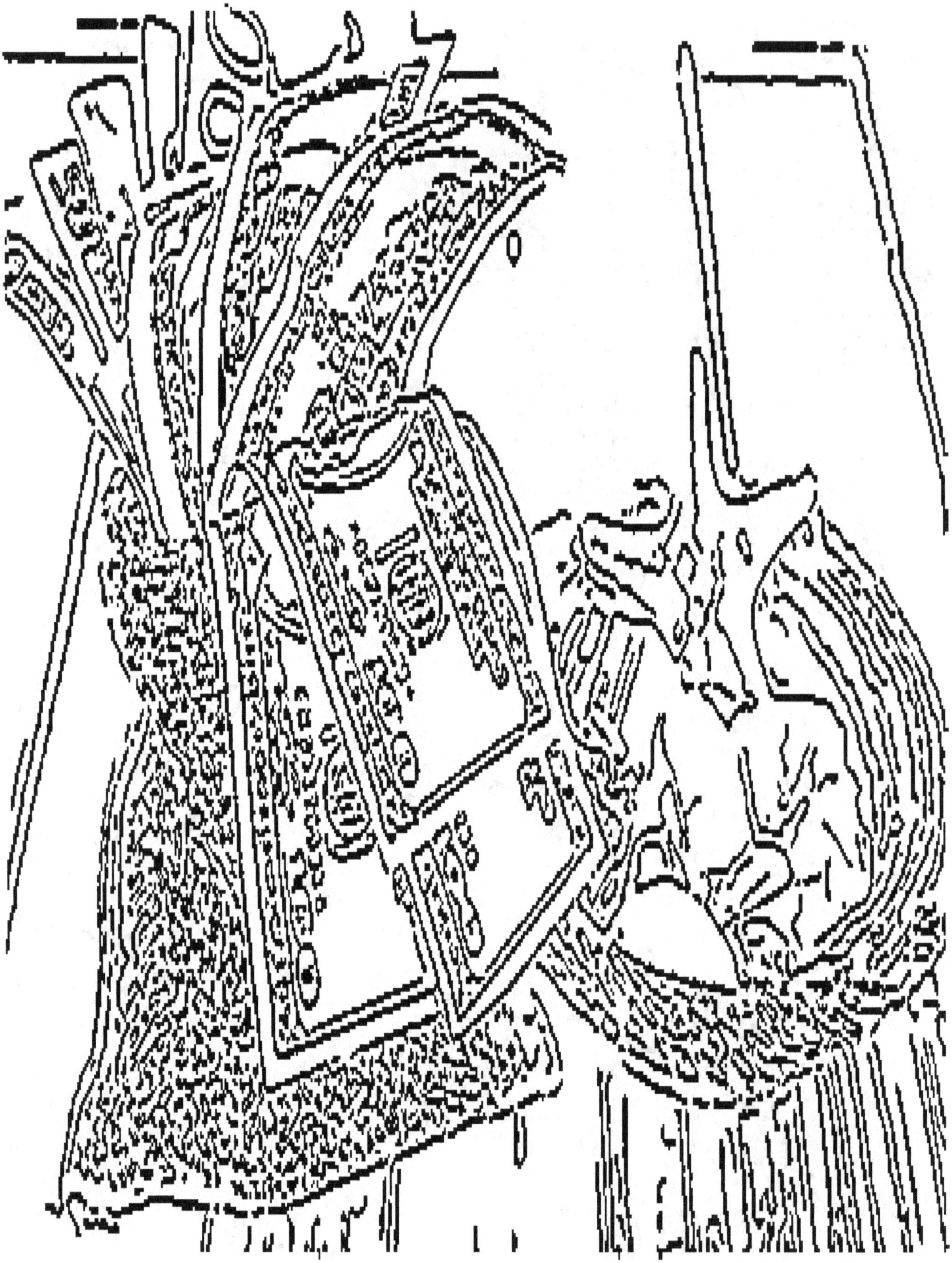

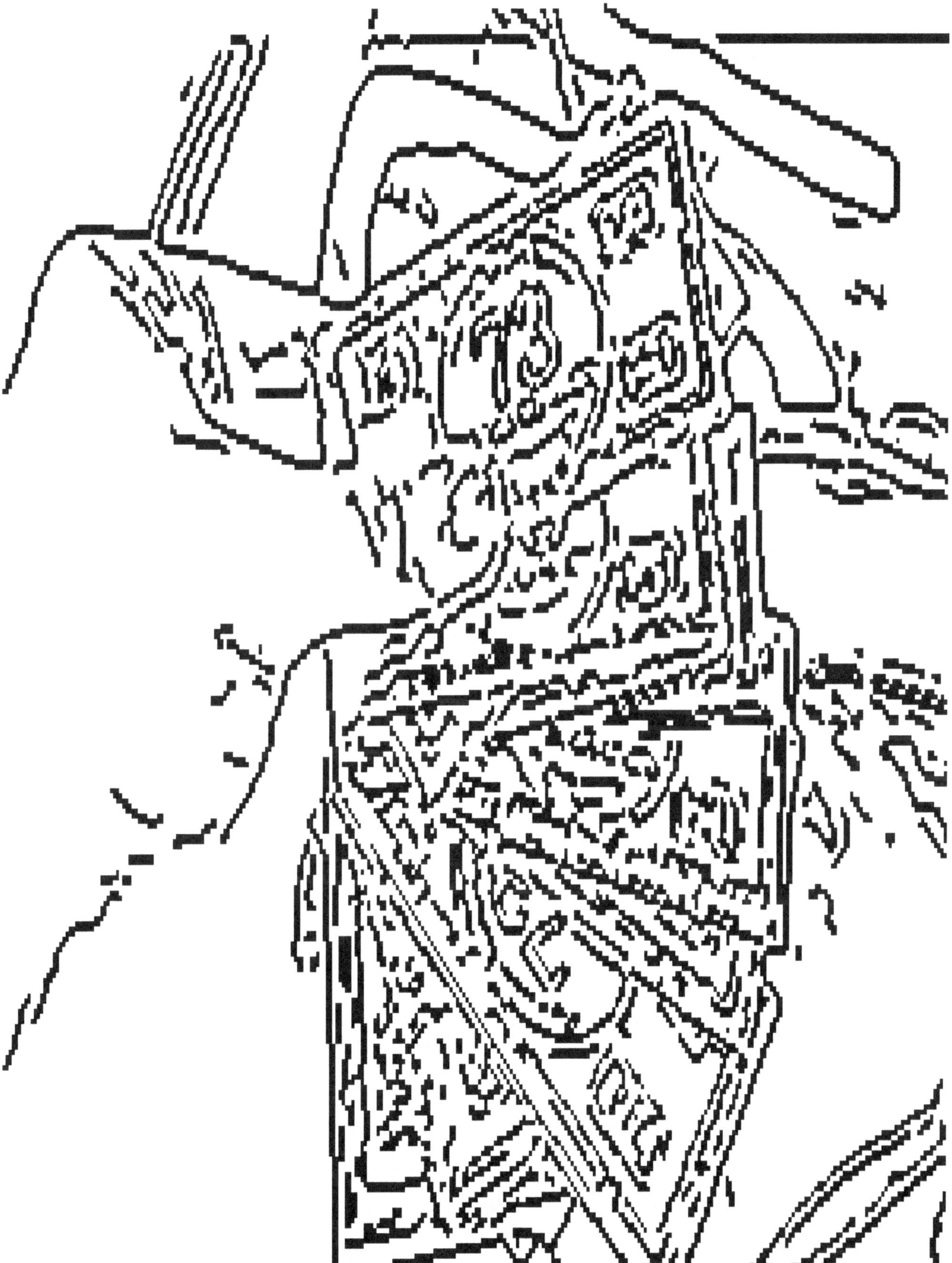

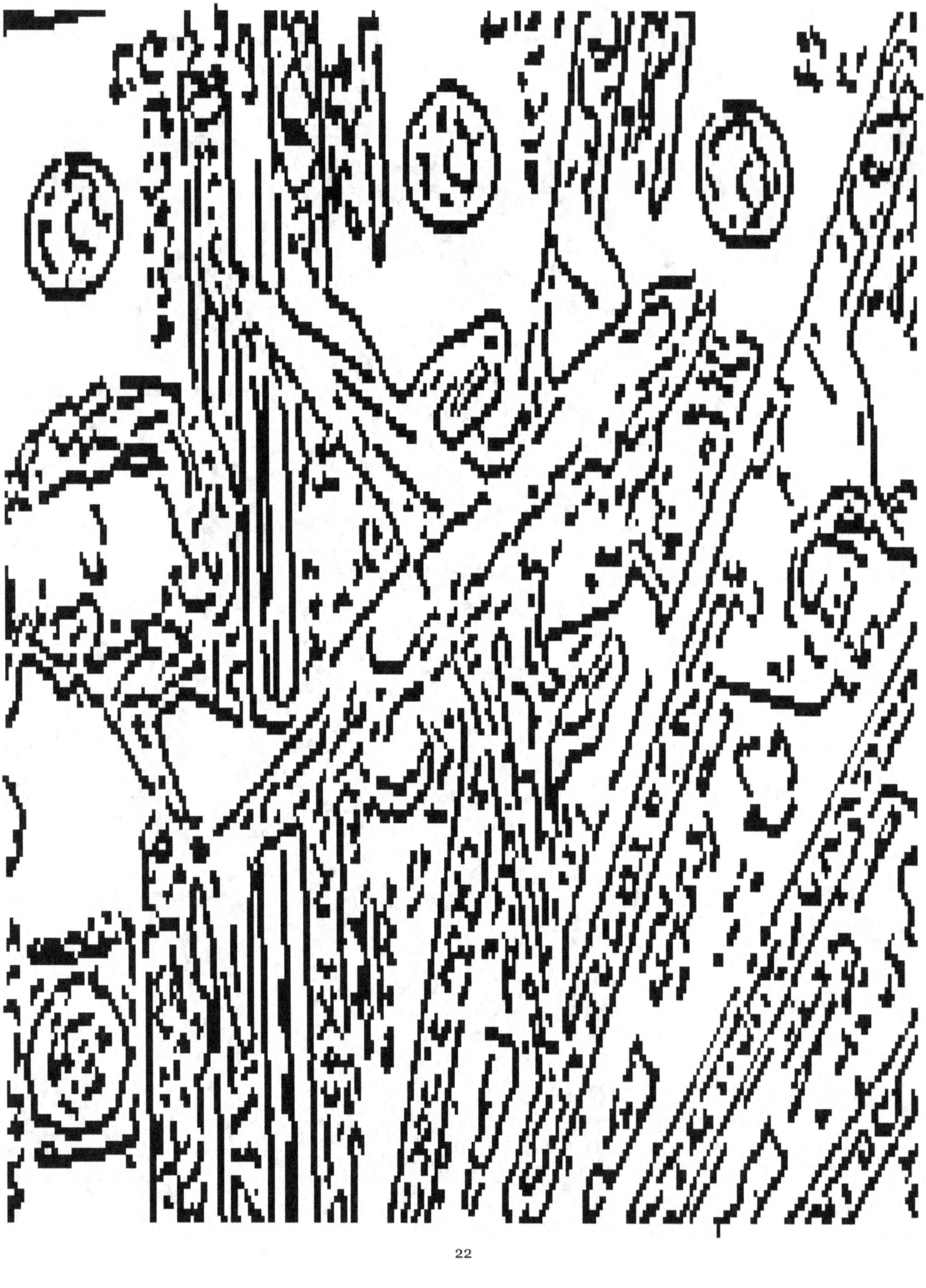

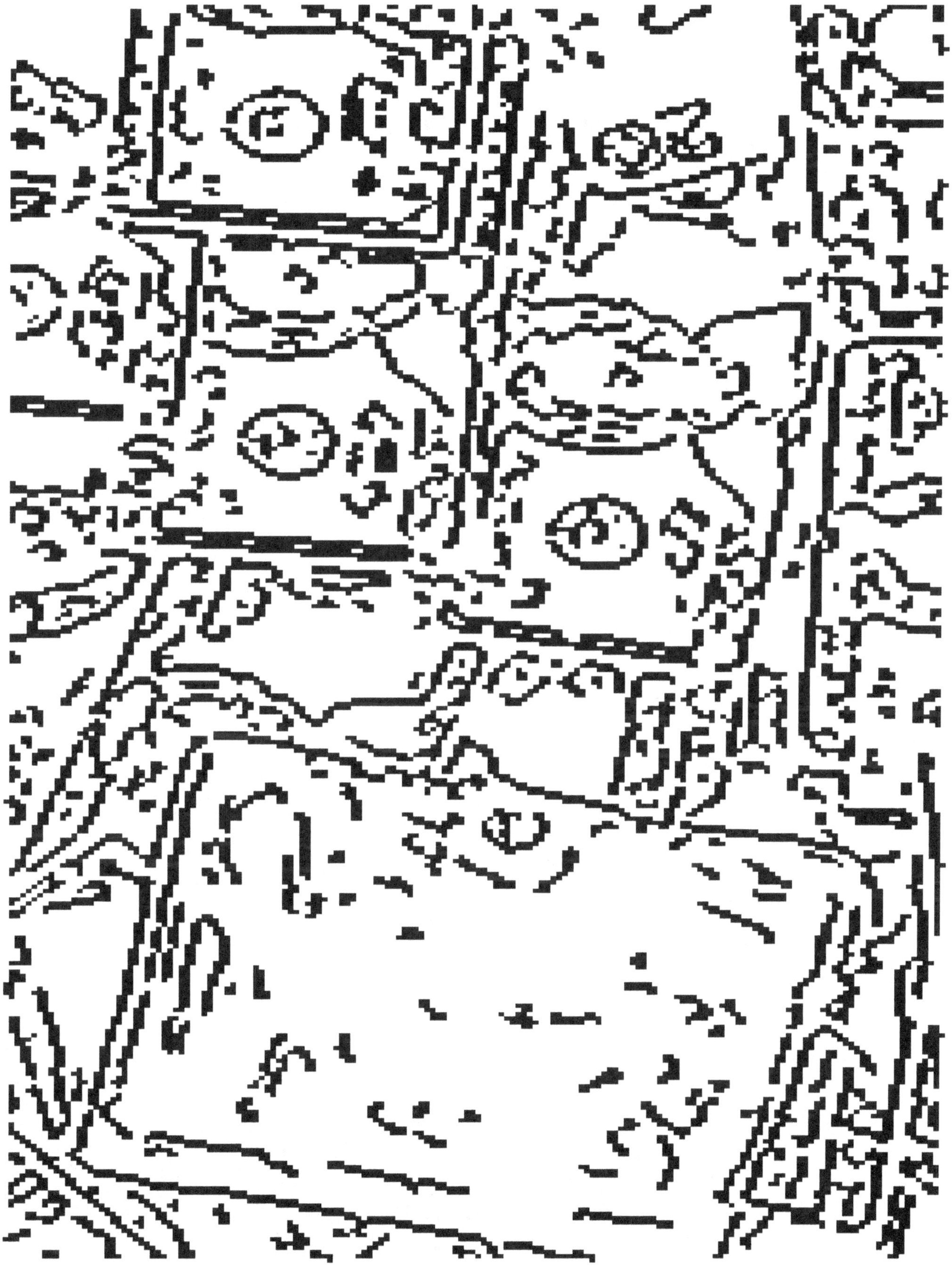

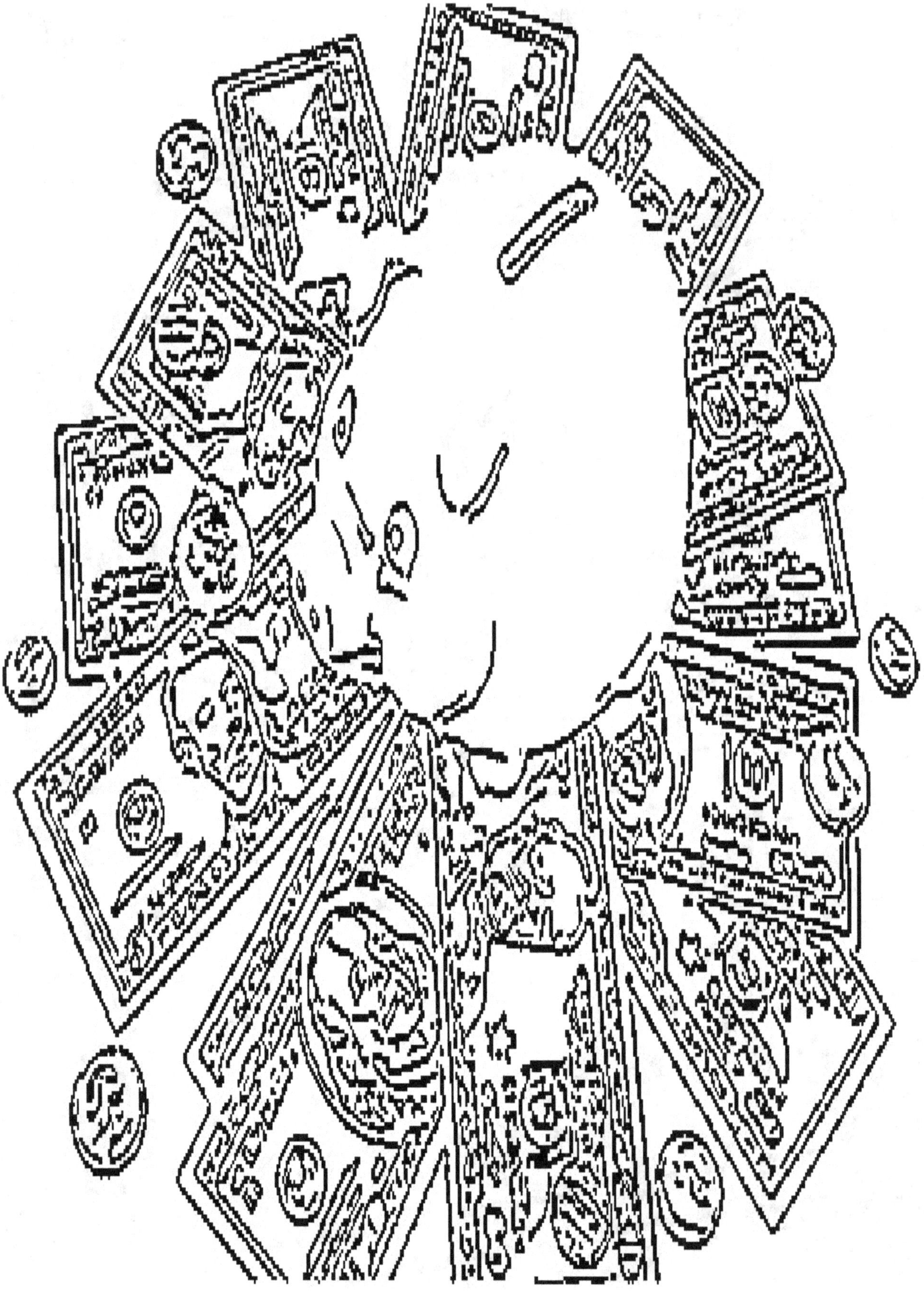

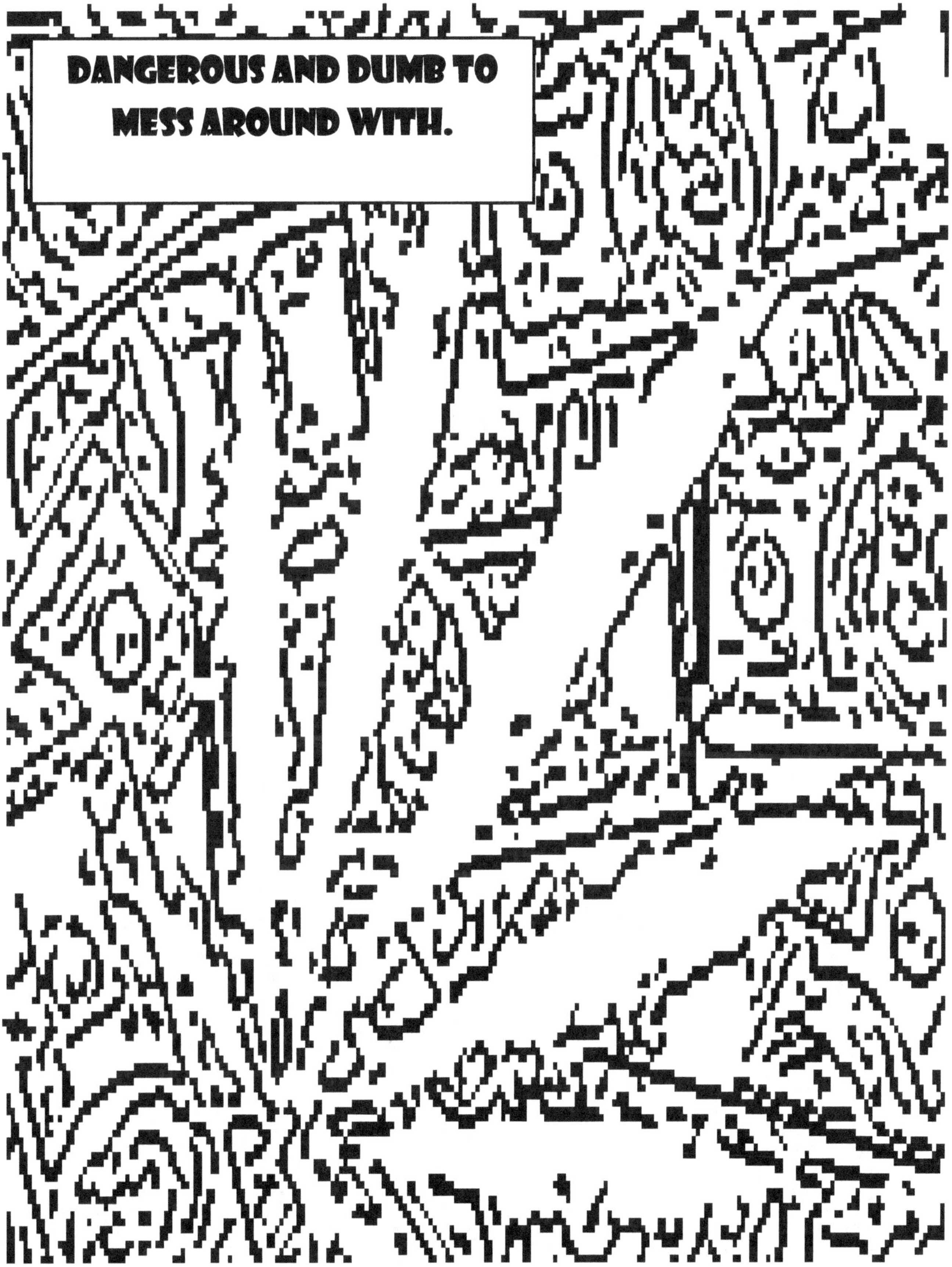
DANGEROUS AND DUMB TO MESS AROUND WITH.

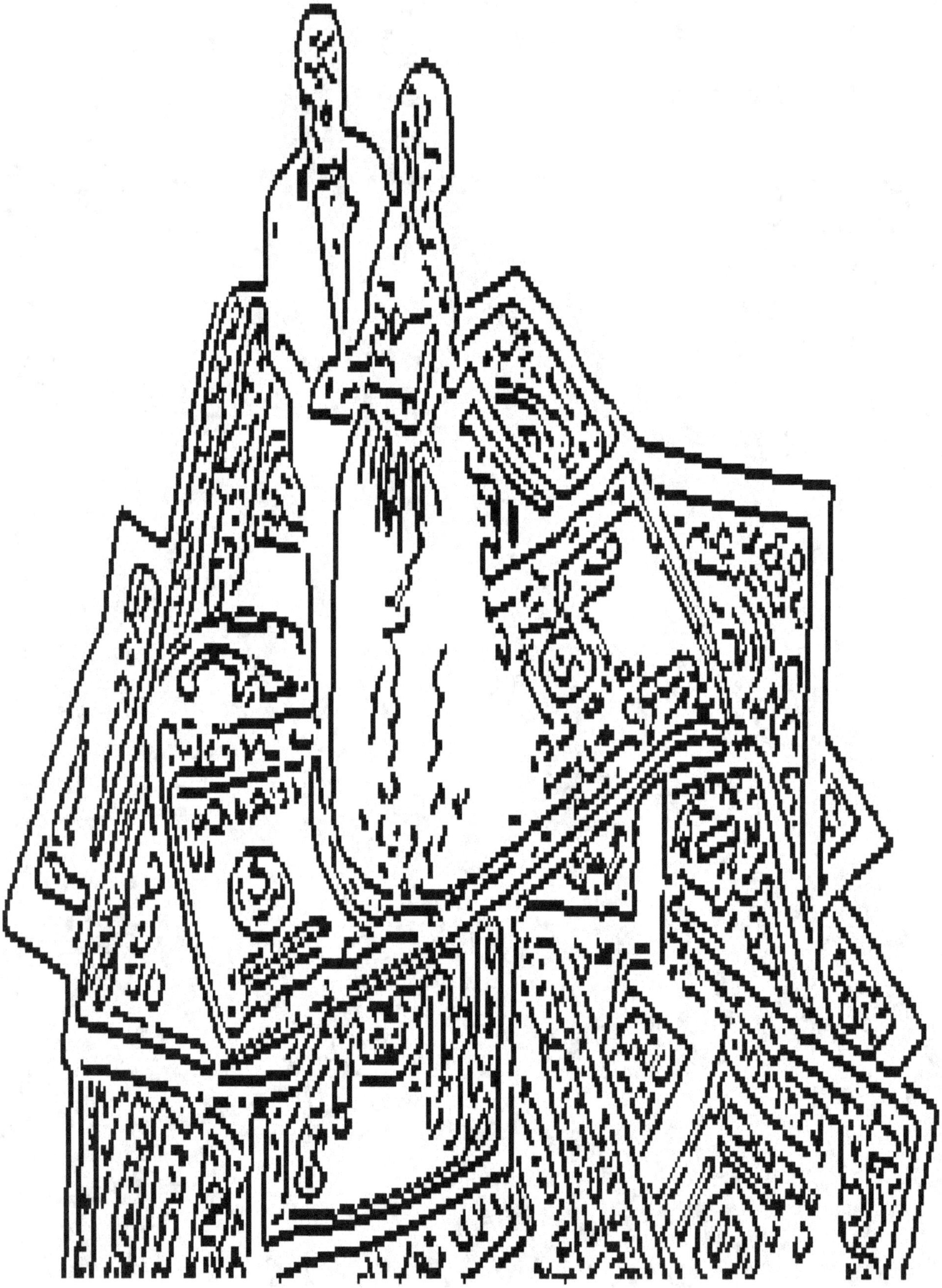

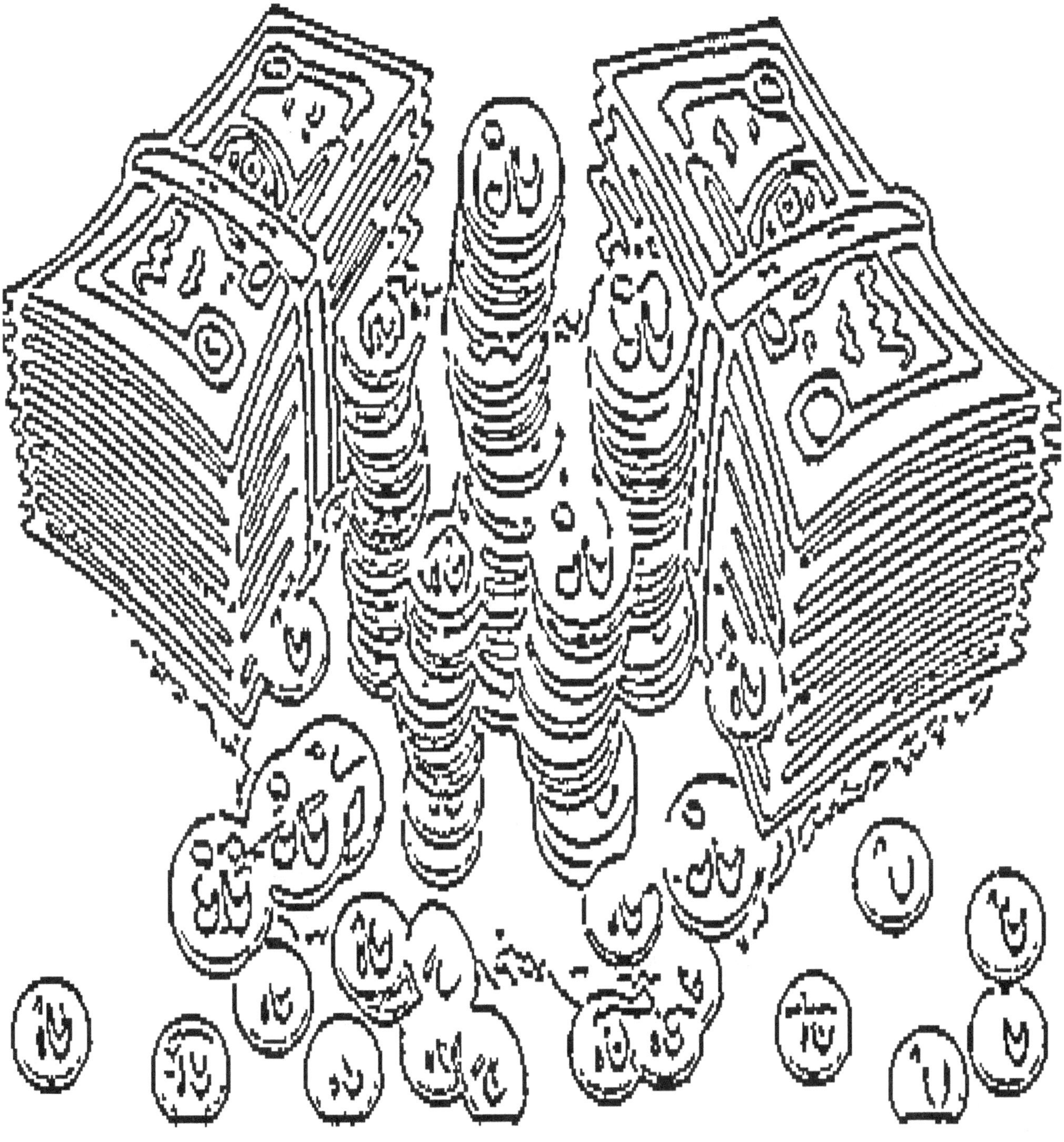

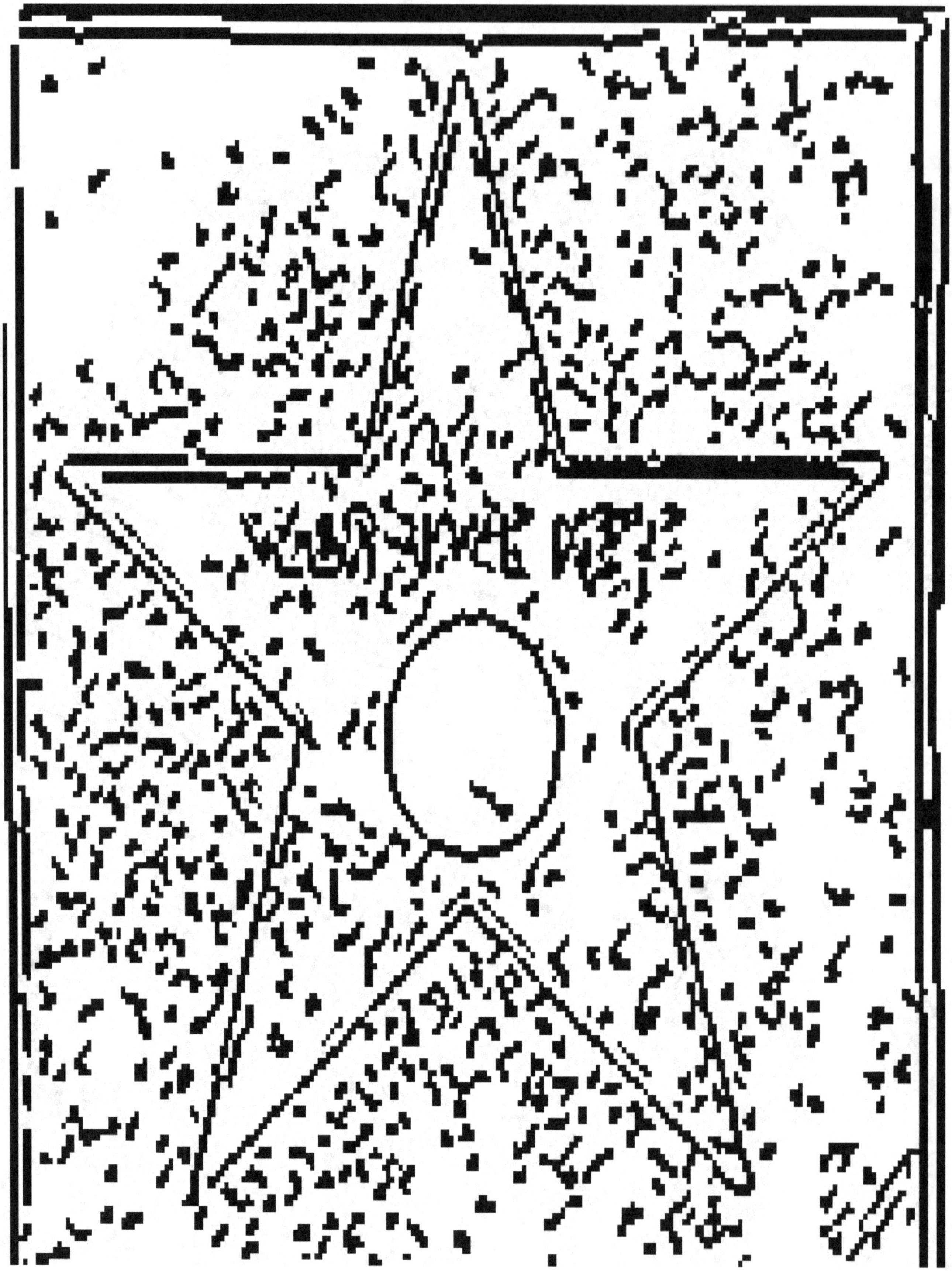

www.ingramcontent.com/pod-product-compliance
Lightning Source LLC
Chambersburg PA
CBHW081316180526
45170CB00007B/2725
* 9 7 8 1 5 4 1 3 9 4 2 6 1 *